An Egg B[ecomes]
a Chic[ken]

By Nick Rebman

SPARKS

Picture Glossary

A chicken lays eggs.

She sits on the eggs.

chicken

Chicks grow in the eggs.

The chicks will grow and grow.

eggs

The chick pokes the shell.

It comes out of the shell.

shell

The chick has wings.

The chick has legs.

The chick has a beak.

chick

The chick eats.

It eats seeds.

seeds

The chick will grow up
to be a big chicken.

chicken

Do You Know?

What is this chicken sitting on?

eggs

chick

shell

seeds